Bon Voyage

Time for Travel

PACKING CHECKLIST

DATE OF TRIP: DURATION:

TRAVEL BUCKET LIST

PLACES I WANT TO VISIT:

_____
_____
_____
_____
_____
_____
_____
_____
_____
_____
_____
_____
_____
_____

THINGS I WANT TO SEE:

_____
_____
_____
_____
_____
_____
_____
_____
_____
_____
_____
_____
_____
_____
_____
_____
_____
_____
_____

TOP 3 DESTINATIONS:

_____
_____
_____

MY TRAVEL JOURNAL

DATE:

WHAT I DID TODAY

HIGHLIGHT OF THE DAY

TRAVEL SNAPSHOT

DOODLES

MY TRAVEL JOURNAL

DATE:

WHAT I DID TODAY

HIGHLIGHT OF THE DAY

TRAVEL SNAPSHOT

DOODLES

MY TRAVEL JOURNAL

DATE:

WHAT I DID TODAY

HIGHLIGHT OF THE DAY

TRAVEL SNAPSHOT

DOODLES

MY TRAVEL JOURNAL

DATE:

WHAT I DID TODAY

HIGHLIGHT OF THE DAY

TRAVEL SNAPSHOT

DOODLES

MY TRAVEL JOURNAL

DATE:

WHAT I DID TODAY

HIGHLIGHT OF THE DAY

TRAVEL SNAPSHOT

DOODLES

MY TRAVEL JOURNAL

DATE:

WHAT I DID TODAY

HIGHLIGHT OF THE DAY

TRAVEL SNAPSHOT

DOODLES

MY TRAVEL JOURNAL

DATE:

WHAT I DID TODAY

HIGHLIGHT OF THE DAY

TRAVEL SNAPSHOT

DOODLES

MY TRAVEL JOURNAL

DATE:

WHAT I DID TODAY

HIGHLIGHT OF THE DAY

TRAVEL SNAPSHOT

DOODLES

MY TRAVEL JOURNAL

DATE:

WHAT I DID TODAY

HIGHLIGHT OF THE DAY

TRAVEL SNAPSHOT

DOODLES

MY TRAVEL JOURNAL

DATE:

WHAT I DID TODAY

HIGHLIGHT OF THE DAY

TRAVEL SNAPSHOT

DOODLES

MY TRAVEL JOURNAL

DATE:

WHAT I DID TODAY

HIGHLIGHT OF THE DAY

TRAVEL SNAPSHOT

DOODLES

MY TRAVEL JOURNAL

DATE:

WHAT I DID TODAY

HIGHLIGHT OF THE DAY

TRAVEL SNAPSHOT

DOODLES

MY TRAVEL JOURNAL

DATE:

WHAT I DID TODAY

HIGHLIGHT OF THE DAY

TRAVEL SNAPSHOT

DOODLES

MY TRAVEL JOURNAL

DATE:

WHAT I DID TODAY

HIGHLIGHT OF THE DAY

TRAVEL SNAPSHOT

DOODLES

MY TRAVEL JOURNAL

DATE:

WHAT I DID TODAY

HIGHLIGHT OF THE DAY

TRAVEL SNAPSHOT

DOODLES

MY TRAVEL JOURNAL

DATE:

WHAT I DID TODAY

HIGHLIGHT OF THE DAY

TRAVEL SNAPSHOT

DOODLES

MY TRAVEL JOURNAL

DATE:

WHAT I DID TODAY

HIGHLIGHT OF THE DAY

TRAVEL SNAPSHOT

DOODLES

MY TRAVEL JOURNAL

DATE:

WHAT I DID TODAY

HIGHLIGHT OF THE DAY

TRAVEL SNAPSHOT

DOODLES

MY TRAVEL JOURNAL

DATE:

WHAT I DID TODAY

HIGHLIGHT OF THE DAY

TRAVEL SNAPSHOT

DOODLES

MY TRAVEL JOURNAL

DATE:

WHAT I DID TODAY

HIGHLIGHT OF THE DAY

TRAVEL SNAPSHOT

DOODLES

MY TRAVEL JOURNAL

DATE:

WHAT I DID TODAY

HIGHLIGHT OF THE DAY

TRAVEL SNAPSHOT

DOODLES

MY TRAVEL JOURNAL

DATE:

WHAT I DID TODAY

HIGHLIGHT OF THE DAY

TRAVEL SNAPSHOT

DOODLES

MY TRAVEL JOURNAL

DATE:

WHAT I DID TODAY

HIGHLIGHT OF THE DAY

TRAVEL SNAPSHOT

DOODLES

MY TRAVEL JOURNAL

DATE:

WHAT I DID TODAY

HIGHLIGHT OF THE DAY

TRAVEL SNAPSHOT

DOODLES

Made in the USA
Middletown, DE
15 June 2021

42347609R00057